Devotions from the Road of Life

Volume 2
Devotions for Caregivers

By Mary Beth Magee

Published by BOTR Press

Copyright 2015

This is a compilation of original works and updates to those works by the author. All rights are reserved. No portion of this book may be copied or redistributed, except for quotation of brief passages for review purposes. Thank you for respecting the hard work of the author.

Cover photo copyright Mary Beth Magee

Except where noted otherwise, all scripture quotes come from the King James Version of the Holy Bible.

Contents

Welcome to Devotions from the Road of Life for Caregivers 1

A Caregiver's Prayer 2

The Basin, the Towel and the Heart 4

Grace and Peace 5

To His Glory 7

Blinded by the Past 9

Morning Will Come 11

He Knows My Name 13

You Can't Escape 14

The Best Laid Plans… 16

The Body Beautiful 18

Frustration 19

Be Kind 20

New Mercies Every Morning 22

Never Forgotten 24

The Battle 26

Afterword: A Word of Comfort when the Job is Finished 28

Acknowledgments 31

About the Author 32

Books by Mary Beth Magee 33

Welcome to Devotions from the Road of Life for Caregivers

Over the course of the last twenty years or so, I've traveled a lot of roads. Some were astounding in their beauty; some were devastating in their cost. None of them were walked alone.

One of the hardest roads I traveled was the path of a caregiver, both personally and professionally. At various points in my life, I've aided with the care of my father, two grandmothers and, longest term, my mother. I've worked in home health care, aiding others in their caregiving. A caregiver experiences many things: physical exhaustion, emotional fatigue, frustration, pain and self-doubt, for example.

Through all of it, God's love carried me. His voice whispered to me of His presence. Moments of joy demonstrated His goodness. He gave me the strength I needed to continue with the job and the contentment of following His will.

If you are a caregiver, or know someone who is, I hope you'll find these messages helpful and encouraging. My prayer for you is to find His face in the face of your patient, find service to Him in the service of your loved one and find His peace when the job is finished.

A Caregiver's Prayer

"And the King shall answer and say unto them, Verily I say unto you, Inasmuch as ye have done it unto one of the least of these my brethren, ye have done it unto me." Matthew 25:40.

I fought my share of battles in the days as I watched my mother decline. Even when she was at her most hurtful and demanding, I had to remind myself I was not only caring for her; I was caring for Jesus through her. I didn't always succeed as well as I desired.

For my fellow caregivers everywhere, as well as myself, I offer this prayer.

A Caregiver's Prayer

Heavenly Father,

Today I look on a face I love without the person I love behind it. Today I seek to provide my loved one's needs, not knowing if I am even recognized. Today I move one day closer to "Farewell."

Please help me to remember the heart and soul now hidden from me. Remind me when I don't have a name in my loved one's eyes, I do have a name in You. Give me strength to do what I must do to provide nourishment and comfort, even when I must do battle with a seeming stranger to do so. Give me patience with the lack of recognition and understanding, with the presence of confusion and fear.

Father, give me cognizance of those flashes of the one who used to be, so I may rejoice in a moment's gift. Give me kindness when the stranger returns. Please remind me that the odd behavior of one I once knew so well comes not from the heart but from the condition now presenting itself.

Make my touch gentle, my voice soft, my thoughts loving. Help me to fight the demons of exhaustion, frustration and depression so I may overcome them in Your mighty Name.

When I grow discouraged, Father, please lift me up. When I grow impatient, please slow me down. Help me at all times to be Your hands and feet to the one who is drawing ever nearer to Your Throne. Remind me that everything I do here, I do to Your glory and as though I do it for You, as well. Remind me to praise You for the opportunity to serve. So many don't get the chance to say "Goodbye," much less show their love through providing care.

Each time I leave the bedside, remind me to say "I love you." This may be the moment when my loved one understands. It may be the last chance I have to say it. It will always be a reminder, even in my darkest moments.

And, dear Father, when the time comes to let go, please remind me we will meet again in Your presence. Comfort me with Your care. Let me hold to the good memories until the day we have the opportunity to make perfect ones, in Your paradise.

In the name of Your Precious Son Jesus I ask these things,
Amen.

The Basin, the Towel and the Heart

"He [Jesus] riseth from supper, and laid aside his garments; and took a towel, and girded himself. After that he poureth water into a bason, and began to wash the disciples' feet, and to wipe them with the towel wherewith he was girded."
John 13:4-5

    Often the example of Jesus washing the feet of the disciples is used as an example of a servant heart. I was content with the explanation until recently. Now I see Jesus' act as an expression of love for the disciples in addition to one of service.

    When my mother was no longer able to bathe alone; I helped her with a sponge bath each day. She washed what she could reach and I washed what she couldn't. The limitation on her reach included her feet. I placed the little wash basin on the floor and she placed her feet in the water, one at a time. I knelt beside her and first washed, then dried each foot.

    The first time she slipped a foot into the pan of warm water, she sighed with pleasure and said, "Oh, that feels so good." I used the washcloth to let water run down her shin and calf, then wiped her leg, from knee to toes. Lifting her foot from the water, I dried it and repeated the process with the other foot. I found myself smiling at her delight.

    And then it struck me: It gave me joy to wash her feet, because I loved giving her the pleasure of the warm water and massage of the washcloth and the resulting clean feet. Because I love her, I love to do things <u>for</u> her. I don't mean to belittle all those theologians who use the basin and towel to demonstrate a servant heart and its importance in the church. I just want to acknowledge the other part of the demonstration, the component which explains the servant one – the love.

At the center of the servant heart is love. We serve those we love for their own sake. We serve those we love for God's sake. Whether we wash their feet or donate money for their relief or serve food at their shelter or however else we may help, we do it for love.

Father, thank you for sending us Your example of perfect love in the form of Your Son. Help us always to reflect Your love in the service we perform. May we always point others toward You, the Source of all love.

Grace and Peace

"Grace be unto you, and peace, from God our Father, and the Lord Jesus Christ. We give thanks to God always for you all, making mention of you in our prayers; Remembering without ceasing your work of faith, and labour of love, and patience of hope in our Lord Jesus Christ, in the sight of God and our Father; Knowing, brethren beloved, your election of God." I Thessalonians 1:1-4

When I moved to California to assist with the care of my mother, I found a dramatically different situation than I expected. She had declined substantially in the five weeks since I had last seen her and was little more than an invalid. I did what I could for her, calling on everything I learned when I worked in home health as a nurse's aide and from my First Aid certification. Yet it seemed so little.

She slept fitfully between her feedings, which were administered through a tube implanted in her stomach. At night, she awakened often, calling for help through the monitor we'd set up in her room with a receiver in mine. Sometimes, it was me she called. Often, it was God. She carried on an unending conversation with Him, asking for relief from the recurring leg cramps we didn't seem to be able to help.

In my own prayers, I asked for strength to be able to provide what she needed; patience to respond in love when she asked the same question for the umpteenth time; gentleness in my touch as I sought to minister to her; and comfort for her. All of those things sound terribly noble, don't they?

Perhaps you won't think so highly of my prayers when I tell you the rest. I very selfishly prayed to have my mother back. Not this frail, suffering woman who tore my heart out with each moan, but the strong, hardworking mother I knew before this decline.

In my heart, I felt she was probably quite close to going home. So each time I approached her bed, I told her I loved her and kissed her head because I didn't know how many more chances I would get. I knew when she left, it wouldn't be forever. I'll see her again one day in glory. But, oh, how I longed to delay the parting!

Paul wasn't specifically talking about my mother in his letter to the church at Thessalonica. Yet it describes her so well. She had worked her entire life in faith and love. What I know of living in grace and counting on God's peace, I learned at her hand. And I wished her grace and peace as she made this final journey. I only hope I can live up to her example in the future.

Is there someone who needs to hear how much you love them? How much they mean to you? Is there someone you love but aren't sure of their spiritual situation? Don't wait – tell them the things they need to hear before time has slipped away. Pray for the confidence and wisdom to do it today.

Father, thank You for the promise of a future together with our loved ones in Your presence. As much as we grieve the decline we witness in the present, we know the future will be glorious. Keep us strong as we serve our loved ones in Your name.

To His Glory

"Commit thy works unto the LORD, and thy thoughts shall be established." Proverbs 16:3

When I first arrived at my sister's house in California to help care for my mother, Mama was not doing well. She required nearly round-the-clock care, was hallucinating, incontinent and pretty helpless.

Eight months later, after scrupulous documentation of her medicines and her reactions to them, trials of other medications and changes in dosage, she improved. We rejoiced in Mama's regained strength and capacity. She was able to attend church services and go to the hairdresser to have her hair done. She could walk around with the aid of her walker and we outfitted the bathtub with a tub transfer bench so she could shower instead of being limited to sponge baths. Wearing incontinence control underwear freed her somewhat from the tyranny of needing to remain close to a toilet. Mama was not self-sufficient, but she was much less dependent on us for moment-to-moment activities than she had been.

In those first few weeks after my arrival, I was worn out from lack of sleep and being unable to relax totally for fear I wouldn't hear Mama if she needed me. I worried about making a mistake in her care through exhaustion. What if I didn't measure her medicine correctly or gave it more often than I should? What if I stumbled while trying to help her ambulate and she fell?

God's still small voice reminded me of many things in those days. He reinforced to me that He was the source of my strength. His love for Mama exceeded mine. He called to my mind the systems of care I had learned so many years ago, first as a candy striper and later as a home health aide. And we made it through those terrible days.

With her improvement, we settled into a routine. The danger became the potential lack of attention to detail which often accompanies routine. How did I overcome this? Each morning, I rose and committed my day's activities to God's glory – the best antidote I know for the mind-numbing effects of the monotony of repetition.

How do you cope with the day-after-day routine of life? Do you seek escape through artificial means such as alcohol or drugs? Do you hide in another world, like video games? Or do you take each step in the company of the God who created you and loves you so much He sent His Son for you. He'll gladly walk with you and make everything you do special because it glorifies Him.

Father, thank you for the opportunity of service to You through serving our fellow man in any honest capacity. Give us strength and wisdom as we work. Take the efforts of our hands and use them to turn people toward You and Your glory.

Blinded by the Past

"And when he was come into his own country, he taught them in their synagogue, insomuch that they were astonished, and said, Whence hath this man this wisdom, and these mighty works? Is not this the carpenter's son? is not his mother called Mary? and his brethren, James, and Joses, and Simon, and Judas? And his sisters, are they not all with us? Whence then hath this man all these things? And they were offended in him. But Jesus said unto them, A prophet is not without honour, save in his own country, and in his own house. And he did not many mighty works there because of their unbelief." Matthew 13:54-58

When I worked as a home-health care provider many years ago, I would sometimes be astounded by how impatient family members could be with an elderly parent or grandparent. How could they be so short-tempered with such a sweet little old person? One day, I think I gained some insight into their behavior.

I was trying to help my mother get dressed. The process became more frustrating because a sinus attack made it difficult for me to bend over long enough to put her socks on her feet. She was slow in lifting her foot toward me. I leaned over, caught her foot and pulled it toward me, annoyed because my head began pounding again before I had the socks in place.

That's when I heard it. The Voice I've come to recognize as God tapping me on the shoulder.

"Is not this the carpenter's son?" Isn't this that skinny kid of Mary's, Jesus? Don't we know his whole family, brothers and sisters and aunts and uncles? The people who had known Jesus as a child were blinded to His adult mission. They couldn't see beyond what they remembered to what was there now.

"Okay, Lord, I get it, but how does that help with Mama?" Then I realized the problem. The memory of the robust, sturdy mother I once knew was blinding me to the present needs of this frail little lady. Mama wasn't *trying* to move more slowly, or cause me problems by not lifting her foot. I was the problem, building expectations on her past abilities instead of dealing with the present.

The challenge comes in discerning what the change means and loving the person, even when we can't love the situation. How can we accept the present and put aside the past? I only know one way – give it to God. I wished my mother didn't need round-the-clock care, and she once again could be the strong woman I remembered, but I loved her, no matter what the circumstance. I prayed for the wisdom to comprehend her current condition and the strength to provide the help she needs.

In the final analysis, God is the One who can perform a litmus test on the soul and identify truth. He can show us the truth, if we allow Him to do so.

It's not too late to make a new start to your relationships. Ask God for wisdom to see the true present in those around you and to veil the past where it would only interfere with the relationship. He can see what we cannot.

Father, thank You for the present. Help us to live in today. Help us to learn from yesterday but not be crippled by it. Give us faith, joy and strength to move forward in our love for You. Amen.

Morning Will Come

"And the LORD smelled a sweet savour; and the LORD said in his heart, I will not again curse the ground any more for man's sake...While the earth remaineth, seedtime and harvest, and cold and heat, and summer and winter, and day and night shall not cease." Genesis 8: 21-22

2:45 a.m. – My mother is calling again. I stumble from my bed in the adjoining room, the one I relocated to so I would be closer to her. I can look out across the shadowed valley through the uncurtained window. How very dark it is without the street lights of suburbia! I can see stars gleaming in the velvet sky and occasionally, the lights of a plane approaching distant Sacramento Airport.

But I can't stop to look for long – Mama needs help. I put aside my sleepiness and shuffle into her room.

When I'm helping her ambulate to her bedside commode chair (or changing her linens because I didn't get there in time), it's easy to give in to exhaustion or frustration. Some of the times, I get there and she doesn't know what she wants or even who I am. There are moments it seems the night will never end and I will be responding to her calls in the darkness forever.

It's at these times I cling to the promise God gave to Noah. Once the ark landed and was unloaded, Noah made a sacrifice of gratitude for God's care and protection. God blessed the sacrifice and made promises as to the future of the earth. One of those promises was "day and night shall not cease."

I know the morning will come, no matter how endless the night seems in the wee hours, no matter how tired I am. My prayer is God will accept my service to my mother as a sacrifice of love to Him and He will find them pleasing.

When the situation seems darkest, remember *"weeping may endure for a night, but joy cometh in the morning."* (Psalm 30: 5b) And morning will come!

Even in the darkest night, Lord, I know You are there. I cling to Your promise of joy in the morning. Thank You for holding me in the palm of Your hand and keeping me close to You, no matter what the circumstances.

He Knows My Name

> *"...the sheep hear his voice: and he calleth his own sheep by name, and leadeth them out. And when he putteth forth his own sheep, he goeth before them, and the sheep follow him: for they know his voice."* John 10: 3b-4

Awake or asleep, Mama calls. If I'm not in the room with her, I hear her on the monitor calling out. Not my name, always. Right now she thinks I'm my late Aunt Louise.

Other times, she calls me Dolores, Katie or Lena, Mutzie or Carrie (other aunts). Occasionally she calls me "Mama." Sometimes, it's a name I don't recognize as family, such as Erma. And sometimes, she calls me by my own name and is quite proud of remembering who I am.

Whatever name she uses, I respond. Occasionally I will tease her with "Louise isn't here. Will I do?" The main thing is her voice is calling out. My mother. I recognize her voice and it gets me moving toward her in response

When I reread Jesus' parable of the sheep, I understood afresh the importance of recognizing the voice doing the calling. I wouldn't respond so quickly to just any voice in the night. And I am so grateful to know that even though Mama doesn't always call me by the right name, He always knows who I am. I am His and He will lead me through whatever is to come.

Do you know the Good Shepherd? He knows you, and would love to count you in His flock. Call on the name of Jesus – He already knows your name!

Thank You, Lord, for loving me enough to know my name and call me Your own. Thank you for loving my mother, too. Please give me wisdom to always recognize Your voice.

You Can't Escape

"The Lord is not slack concerning his promise, as some men count slackness; but is longsuffering to us-ward, not willing that any should perish, but that all should come to repentance." II Peter 3:9

My mother has become something of an escape artist, in spite of our best efforts. She has fallen several times while trying to get out of bed during the night. My sister and I have tried any number of ways to keep her safe.

We keep a baby monitor in her room so she can call for assistance if she needs to get up during the night. She sleeps in a hospital bed with side rails to try to keep her from getting up and wandering around without someone to help her stay upright.

She evades the monitor by not saying anything as she sneaks out of the bed. She takes advantage of the foot-long gap between the end of the rail and the foot of the bed to slither, snakelike, out into the room. On occasion, she tries to slip out under the rail, resulting in being caught like a fox in a trap – unable to get out or go back into the bed.

Some mornings, I come into the room to find her sitting on the edge of the bed, arms resting atop the rail and feet dangling as though she were sitting at a desk. One morning, I found her on her knees, with her shoulders wedged between the rail and the frame. And some heart-stopping mornings I find her on the floor. She made good her escape from the bed, only to find her strength spent.

God has blessed us. Mama sinks to the floor, rather than falling, on most occasions. She has suffered no broken bones, only some minor abrasions and bruising. But we fear the time of a solid fall or a piece of furniture in the way. So we continue trying to protect her and she continues trying to escape.

I can't help but be reminded of God and His love for us. We keep trying to escape His love. He keeps opening His arms to bring us back to His protection. We have His promise to keep making the offer of eternal life to us, because He is faithful and unwilling to let any of us go to eternal death.

Mama has the underlying cause of dementia to spur her attempts to "escape." What reason can any of us use to justify trying to escape God? Yet we do, more often than we would probably admit. Each time we do what we find expedient rather than what He has told us is right, we are trying to escape.

Father, please forgive me when I fight Your will and try to do things my own way. Remind me of Your constant love and care. Help me to rest in the knowledge of Your goodness. And thank You so much for watching over Mama!

The Best Laid Plans...

"But a certain Samaritan, as he journeyed, came where he was: and when he saw him, he had compassion on him, And went to him, and bound up his wounds, pouring in oil and wine, and set him on his own beast, and brought him to an inn, and took care of him. And on the morrow when he departed, he took out two pence, and gave them to the host, and said unto him, Take care of him; and whatsoever thou spendest more, when I come again, I will repay thee." Luke 10: 33-35

When I arrived to help care for my mother, I envisioned after-work hours spent in writing as I sat near her, ready to meet any need she may have. My sister had reported Mama did little more than sleep between her feedings (which took place through a percutaneous endoscopic gastrostomy - or PEG - tube).

Reality was somewhat different than my imaginings. I didn't find a job. Mama only slept intermittently (even at night!). She talked in her sleep, often crying out as though in distress or pain. She required help ambulating to and from her bedside commode chair. Sometimes we could convince her to walk a little more, into the living room or perhaps into her bathroom for a quick "spit bath" in the sink.

Occasionally, Mama developed pain in her legs or feet. We used lavender oil or a chamomile based cream to massage the ailing part. Sometimes she just craved the human touch of someone holding her hand.

She imagined strange people in the room, and wanted me to order them out or check on what they are doing. There were "accidents" requiring her bed to be changed, sometimes numerous times a day. The resultant loads of laundry had to be washed, dried, folded and put away.

Another problem arose from the failure of the muscles in her esophagus, the reason the PEG tube was installed. The tube took care of getting nutrition into her, but it couldn't help her feeling of needing to burp. We tried any number of antics to dislodge reluctant air bubbles: walking, getting up and down, patting her on the back, and anything else we could think of to try to clear the bubble.

These interruptions came without warning. My concentration got broken; whatever I was working on got set aside. Most of the writing I planned to get done was still waiting for me.

I wonder if the Samaritan had plans for his day, on the road between Jerusalem and Jericho? Whatever they were, he put them aside to care for the man who had fallen among thieves. In putting his own plans on hold, he kept the appointment God had for him. The compassion he demonstrated has come to mean someone who cares above and beyond expectations – the Good Samaritan. Each time my plans get rearranged, I try to remember the Good Samaritan and open my heart to God's plans.

Father, thank you for having the Master Plan. Please forgive me those times when I consider my own plans to be the most important things in the world. Help me to look to You for the right "next step" and not my own thoughts.

The Body Beautiful

"I will praise thee; for I am fearfully and wonderfully made: marvellous are thy works; and that my soul knoweth right well." Psalm 139: 14

A caregiver faces many issues. Beyond the physical demands of helping someone to rise from a bed or chair are the emotional demands of assisting in nutrition or personal hygiene.

For my mother, meals consisted of liquids hung in a gravity-feed bag called a kangaroo pouch. The nutritional liquid entered through a tube into a valve implanted in her stomach wall – a percutaneous endoscopic gastrostomy *(PEG)* tube. Each feeding and/or dose of medication required exposing her upper abdomen for access to the tube.

Because she was weak and had poor balance, Mama required help bathing and even going to the bathroom. She lamented having to let me see her body, embarrassed by the lack of privacy and modesty she experienced. Although I tried to be mindful of her dignity, sometimes we both fell prey to giggling fits as I washed and dry her feet, particularly between her toes. Neither of us is in a very dignified position at that moment!

Through all of this, I was amazed by her. Her limbs were wrapped in crepe-like skin, slack against out-of-tone muscles. Yet I could sometimes convince her to work to pull herself up, to walk back and forth to try to build her strength. Although she'd given birth to four daughters, her stomach was still flat, although the skin was not smooth. I marveled at the grip of her gnarled hands, as we locked forearms to steady her gait.

How wondrous is the human body! Even as it winds down, it is a thing of amazing beauty. The gentleness of her touch and the comfort of her embrace were still delights. Her smile, when I could entice one from her, was as warm as June sunshine.

One day I had to say farewell to her body. The truth which comforted me is, her soul goes on and we will meet again in glory. How marvelous, Lord! How wondrously marvelous!

Father, I thank you for the love You put into creating each of us. We are each beautiful in our own way, by Your design. Help us to see Your creation in each other at all stages of life, and to appreciate each other in Your Name.

Frustration

"In my distress I cried unto the LORD, and he heard me. Deliver my soul, O LORD..." Psalm 120:1-2a

My mother had good days and she had bad days. When she had a bad day, it meant I would have a bad day as well. I loved her dearly, but sometimes she exhausted me with her demands.

She was too cold, but the covers I put on her were too heavy.

She asked for water while I was balancing a measuring cup and her liquid medication, and got upset when I stopped to put down the cup and bottle to get her water.

She didn't like the clothes I picked out for her to wear, but got angry and accused me of being 'mean' to her when I suggested she pick out something she would prefer.

She got restless and went from bed to chair to bed, up and down, a restless wraith haunting my soul with her discomfort.

Do I sound as though I'm whining? In a way, I am. I got frustrated with not being able to fix things for her, to make everything all right again. My frustration expressed itself in a 'poor me pity party.'

Finally, I did what I should have done in the first place. I remembered to turn it over to God. He felt Mama's pain and restlessness. He knew my aggravation. He loved us both. When I asked, He calmed my heart and gave me an added dose of patience to deal with Mama's moods.

Do you have a source of frustration, a problem you can't seem to solve? Cry out to Him. He will hear and help. Perhaps He will calm the storm, as He did for the disciples. Perhaps He will calm you.

Thank you, Father, for the peace You bring us. Help us to remember where to turn when the problems mount and aggravation grows. Thank you for loving us even when we are most unlovable. Thank you for hearing our call.

Be Kind

"Let all bitterness, and wrath, and anger, and clamor, and railing, be put away from you, with all malice: and be ye kind one to another, tenderhearted, forgiving each other, even as God also in Christ forgave you." Ephesians 4:31-32, American Standard Version

As my mother's dementia deepened and she descended further into the oblivion of Alzheimer's, she became increasingly argumentative and demanding. She "saw" things and people and got quite upset when we told her there wasn't anything or anyone there. She had trouble completing sentences.

Verse 31 of Ephesians 4 is almost a litany of her behavior: bitterness, wrath, anger, clamor, railing and malice. Not much I did was right, according to her evaluation. Her pillows were too high, then too low. The room was too cold, then too hot. Her clothes were too big or too tight. And so the days passed.

As she went on and on, the temptation was to respond in kind, to stand up to her and give her as good as she gave me. I am ashamed to say there are moments when I yielded to the temptation and heard myself scolding back at her, considerably louder than I ought to have addressed her.

Then I remembered the verse which was so often a memory verse: *"And be ye kind one to another, tenderhearted, forgiving one another, even as God for Christ's sake hath forgiven you."* The King James Version was the one we used back when I was a Sunday School child. Ephesians 4:32 popped into my head and I remembered I should be tenderhearted toward the stranger who inhabited my mother's body.

There are two important parts to the verse. The first is clear; we should be kind to each other. The second part is equally clear and equally important. Forgive as we have been forgiven. Oops.

There were times when I was full of those verse 31 feelings, too. I was angry because my mother was in such a condition and I was helpless against it. I clamored about the unfairness of being laid off at my age and how useless I felt to be unemployed. Yet God, through the love He bears His Son, forgave me those unkind feelings. How could I do less for my mother?

Take time to be kind to someone today, someone who doesn't seem to deserve your kindness. I can promise you they need it. Just as you have received the kindness of God's forgiveness because you needed it.

Father, we thank You for Your great kindness which You give to us through Christ Jesus. Help us to pass the kindness along to others, and to forgive as we have been forgiven.

New Mercies Every Morning

"This I recall to my mind, therefore have I hope. It is of the LORD's mercies that we are not consumed, because his compassions fail not. They are new every morning: great is thy faithfulness. The LORD is my portion, saith my soul; therefore will I hope in him. The LORD is good unto them that wait for him, to the soul that seeketh him. It is good that a man should both hope and quietly wait for the salvation of the LORD." Lamentations 3: 21-26

This morning I awoke to one of those glorious autumn mornings, the ones I love so much. I went outside to temperatures in the mid-50s, a bright blue sky with a scattering of interesting clouds and a hint of someone burning logs in their fireplace on the air. South Mississippi had its best fall attitude in place, promising a beautiful Thanksgiving.

I breathed a quick "Thank You, Lord," as I helped my mother to the car. We were on our way to a medical appointment for her and the beautiful day made transporting her much easier.

Her doctor replaced her old, worn out PEG tube (the device through which she eats) with a new type. This one doesn't require the pain shots and effort which always accompanied changing out the old style appliance. The newer technology promises easier replacements in the future, as well. Another "Thank You, Lord" crosses my lips.

Every morning brings new advances, new knowledge in the medical realm. I choose to see these advances as evidence of the observation of Lamentations' author. God's goodness, His mercies are new every day. They never run dry, go "out of stock" or get stale. They aren't on backorder, the wrong size or the wrong color. His love for us is constant, never ending and perfect in its constancy.

The official holiday season starts in two days. Unofficially, it's already underway. Amid the food, gifts, festivities, stress and rush, don't forget to rest and "hope and quietly wait." Take a moment or two each day to acknowledge those mercies God sends your way. You may even find yourself more aware and cognizant of them!

Father, we thank You that You're already blessing us each morning when we rise, even before we ask. Please accept our gratitude and remind us to express it when we get distracted. You are our hope, our salvation, our joy. Amen.

Never Forgotten

"How long wilt thou forget me, O LORD? for ever? how long wilt thou hide thy face from me? How long shall I take counsel in my soul, having sorrow in my heart daily? how long shall mine enemy be exalted over me? Consider and hear me, O LORD my God: lighten mine eyes, lest I sleep the sleep of death; Lest mine enemy say, I have prevailed against him; and those that trouble me rejoice when I am moved. But I have trusted in thy mercy; my heart shall rejoice in thy salvation. I will sing unto the LORD, because he hath dealt bountifully with me." Psalm 13

Deep sadness covered me for a time during my mother's illness. I felt as though we *had* been forgotten in God's plan.

We were still in California when red streaks appeared under my mother's left arm on August 9, 2011. I feared infection of some sort and called her doctor immediately. They had me bring her into the office. The nurse practitioner and doctor consulted over the growing streaks and had me take her across the street to the emergency room.

In the ER, they ran tests and scans. The results showed enlargement of her lymph nodes and tiny but suspicious masses in her left breast. Their preliminary diagnosis was suspected breast cancer and she was referred to a surgeon for a biopsy.

Her surgeon, a giant of a man who teased her as though she was his sister, had done the surgery to implant her PEG tube. I was glad she had a familiar face to accompany her on this journey. He came out of the surgery with grim news. My mother did indeed have breast cancer.

Because of her age and health complications, surgery wasn't a good option. Fortunately, her cancer was a type with a good response record to treatment with tamoxifen. One more pill joined her daily regimen.

As David cried out so long ago, "I have trusted in thy mercy...I will sing unto the Lord, because he hath dealt bountifully with me." God dealt bountifully with my mother, as well. The incisions from her biopsy healed well and with minimal pain. The tumors responded well to treatment and became undetectable within a few months. She suffered no side effects from the drug during the time she took it.

The journey began with the streaks and ended twenty months later in south Mississippi when she succumbed to the complications of Alzheimer's and the collapse of her digestive system. The breast cancer tumors remained undetectable.

Father, thank You for the bountiful love You pour over us. Thank You for loving my mother and showing her Your love throughout her life. Thank You for promising us a grand reunion in Your presence someday.

The Battle

In the darkness of the night, questions assail me.

How can I keep going, when all I kept going for is gone?

What can I do when what I have done for so long no longer needs doing?

Where do I place my efforts, when the one I worked so long to help has left me behind?

My tears pour out in a river of defeat and grief, my best efforts shattered ruins of failure.

In the quiet of my heart's darkness comes the answer.

I will never leave you or forsake you. You are not alone.

The one you love is safe within my arms,

Gone from your sight but not your heart or my care.

You will be together again.

Carry on, there is other work for you to do in my kingdom.

The light of my love will guide you on, if you will only follow.

Be comforted.

This victory is won.

Claim it and rejoice.

This verse poured out of my heart in the wake of my mother's passing. It first appeared in the Inspire Christian Writers anthology, *Inspire Victory*, in March of 2014.

Afterword: A Word of Comfort when the Job is Finished

Chances are you've lost the one for whom you were caring. They've gone home and left you behind to carry on without them. You've spent a lot of time and energy on a job with little hope of a happy ending, but you did the job well. Now the pain is what's left and the hours are empty, without your special someone to care for.

As you face this loss, those of us around you have trouble knowing what to say. We want to offer you words of comfort and condolence, to make this trauma easier for you. We just don't always know how.

I wish I could tell you everything will be fine and normal.
The truth is, things will never be the same again.

I wish I could tell you the hurt will go away.
The truth is, the pain will ease but the scar will not vanish.

I wish I could tell you I knew why this happened.
The truth is, I don't but I know Who does.

In this moment, when the pain is raw and new, a fresh wound on your heart, you don't want platitudes or empty promises. You want, you need the truth. So here it is.

God loves you and He loves your absent loved one. More than anything in the world, He wants your well-being. And the best, most wonderful place anyone can be is with the One who loves best.

In order to get to that perfect place, we have to take a journey through life. The path can be torturous, but we have a guide who will bring us through. He's made the trip before and He will show us the way.

"Thomas saith unto him, Lord, we know not whither thou goest; and how can we know the way? Jesus saith unto him, I am the way, the truth, and the life: no man cometh unto the Father, but by me. If ye had known me, ye should have known my Father also: and from henceforth ye know him, and have seen him." John 14:5-7

Because of God's great love for us, He sent His Son, Jesus Christ, to pay the debt for our sins. Jesus promised us He was making ready a wonderful destination for us to someday inhabit with Him.

"Let not your heart be troubled: ye believe in God, believe also in me. In my Father's house are many mansions: if it were not so, I would have told you. I go to prepare a place for you. And if I go and prepare a place for you, I will come again, and receive you unto myself; that where I am, there ye may be also." John 14:1-3

As a Christian, your loved one has gone ahead to be with Him. In God's perfect timing, you will join them there, if you are also saved. We have His word.

There is no sadness you can know that Jesus has not felt, too. There is no sorrow you can feel He has not experienced as well. You do not travel this lonely road alone; He goes with you.

"Yea, though I walk through the valley of the shadow of death, I will fear no evil: for thou art with me; thy rod and thy staff they comfort me." Psalm 23:4

The joy of reunion will be so much sweeter when you know you will be together with your loved ones in His presence for all eternity. Take comfort in this knowledge: the best is yet ahead. While you may experience dark days now, the sunshine of God's love still shines and the brightness of His goodness awaits you.

No, I can't tell you everything will be fine and normal, or the hurt will go away. I can't explain why this happened.

But I can tell you God knows and He is with you. His love never fails and no one can interrupt it.

"It is Christ that died, yea rather, that is risen again, who is even at the right hand of God, who also maketh intercession for us. Who shall separate us from the love of Christ? shall tribulation, or distress, or persecution, or famine, or nakedness, or peril, or sword?" Romans 8:34b-35

We are His. Whether we are here on earth, or in His presence in glory, we are His forever.

The pain is for a little while. The joy is eternal. What a promise! What a loving God! What an amazing Savior! Take heart, and hold on for the day of reunion. Keep your eyes on Jesus and your heart hopeful. I pray you will allow the comfort of His love to help you through this difficult time.

Acknowledgments

No one grows up asking for the job of someday caring for an infirm family member. I'm no different; I didn't find the job, the job found me.

Giving good care requires a lot of knowledge. I learned from many compassionate instructors along the way.

My first inspiration came from an adult cousin who worked as a nursing supervisor at a major hospital. Thanks, Pat.

My first teachers were on staff at the little neighborhood hospital in New Orleans where I served as a Candy Striper. Mrs. Johnson, Jonesy and Mr. Moore took the time to teach me little techniques to provide care for a patient as a person, not just a case. A soothing massage can give more relief than a drug when the patient feels lonely.

Later, I asked questions whenever I was in a caregiving environment. Physicians (sometimes), nurses (always!) and lab personnel all shared their expertise within legal boundaries and helped me grow as a caregiver.

As a home health aide I had access to training opportunities and I took any I could get.

My degree in Psychology included courses in adult learning and the psychological issues facing older adults. Thanks to all of my professors who were willing to address one more question about the aging process.

To the health care professionals who cared for my loved ones and were willing to hear me out about my concerns, you have my eternal gratitude. Our goals were the same and we became a team.

For my family members who contributed in whatever ways they could along the way, thank you. I love you.

To Trudy, who gave me a way to bring my Mama home before she died, you are the sister of my heart. Thank you seems so little to say.

Finally, to God, who gave the strength I needed to keep going and provided the resources along the road, I give the praise and glory.

About the Author

Mary Beth Magee moved to California in late 2008 to care for her mother. The ups and downs of her mother's condition over the next 4-1/2 years tested her skill as a caregiver in many ways.

Her mother suffered from COPD, scoliosis, osteoporosis, achalasia (the esophageal problem which led to the PEG tube), Alzheimer's and finally, breast cancer. She went home to be with the Lord shortly after her eighty-sixth birthday.

In September of 2012, Magee was able to bring her mother back home to the South. In her last months, she was able to visit with her brothers and sister and many nieces and nephews, as well as her adopted family and friends. God blessed her with lucidity during those visits and provided many treasured memories.

Some of these devotions have appeared previously on Internet sites over the last few years in earlier forms. They have been updated where appropriate.

Magee writes for several Internet sites and Southern Senior, a regional quarterly magazine. She also writes cozy Christian mystery with a Southern accent.

She is available for presentations on writing and inspirational topics. Her brochure is available on her website.

Email Mary Beth Magee at MaryBethMageeWrites@gmail.com. Visit her website at www.LOL4.net.

Books by Mary Beth Magee

Death in the Daylilies, An (LOL)^4 Mystery

Devotions from the Road of Life: Volume 1 Hitting the Road

Songs of Childhood, Echoes of Years

Anthology Appearances:

Not Your Mother's Book on Being a Stupid Kid

Not Your Mother's Book on Being a Parent

Picayune Writers Group 2014 Anthology

Inspire Victory

Inspire Promise

Chicken Soup for the Soul: Thanks to My Mom

Made in the USA
San Bernardino, CA
17 May 2016